BROKEN WORLD

Broken World

POEMS BY JOSEPH LEASE

COFFEE HOUSE PRESS

MINNEAPOLIS

Coffee House Press books are available to the trade through our primary distributor, Consortium Book Sales & Distribution, www.cbsd.com or (800) 283-3572. For personal orders, catalogs, or other information, write to: info@coffeehousepress.org.

Coffee House Press is a nonprofit literary publishing house. Support from private foundations, corporate giving programs, government programs, and generous individuals helps make the publication of our books possible. We gratefully acknowledge their support in detail in the back of this book. To you and our many readers around the world, we send our thanks for your continuing support.

"'Broken World' (For James Assatly)" appeared in *The Best American Poetry 2002* (Scribner), edited by Robert Creeley and David Lehman. Grateful acknowledgment is made to the editors of the journals in which these poems first appeared: *Colorado Review:* "'Broken World' (For James Assatly)" and "Soul-making"; *First Intensity:* "The History of Our Death"; *New American Writing:* "Ghosts," "Little Lightning Bolt," and "Prayer, Broken Off"; *Volt:* "Cy Twombly"; *Xantippe:* "Free Again" (a chapbook/special supplement); eleven poems from "Free Again" appeared in *Bay Poetics* (Faux Press, 2006), edited by Stephanie Young; "'Broken World' (For James Assatly)" and "The History of Our Death" appeared in the chapbook *My Sister Life* (Jensen/Daniels, 2001).

Library of Congress Cataloging-in-Publication Data

Lease, Joseph.
Broken world : poems / Joseph Lease.
p. cm.
ISBN-13: 978-1-56689-198-1 (alk. paper)
ISBN-10: 1-56689-198-1 (alk. paper)
I. Title.
PS3562.E255B76 2007
811'.54—DC22
2006038348

5 7 9 8 6 4
Printed in the United States

FOR DONNA

ONE

TWO

One

GHOSTS

the word for dawn
    is *others*

the word for light
    is *freefall*

the word for hand
    is *others*

the word for dawn
    is *sister*

her weeds
    her bridge

her clay-blue sky her wind
    and rain her friends

her house
    her stream

of ghosts
    her horses

were her beauty
her horses

her stories
the word for dawn

is *others*
the word for light

is *nothing*

"BROKEN WORLD"
(FOR JAMES ASSATLY)

1

faith and rain
            brightness falls

            blank as glass
                        brightness falls

            until he

can't bend
            light anymore.

            Won't be stronger. Won't be water.
Won't be dancing or floating berries.
Won't be a year. Won't be a song.
Won't be taller. Won't be accounted
a flame. Won't be a boy. Won't be
any relation to the famous rebel.

You are with me
        and I shatter

everyone who
        hates you.

Arrows on water;
        you are with me—

rain on snow—
        and I shatter

everyone who
        hates you.

2

To be a man, to be, to try. I hate the word *man*. I'm not crazy about the word *husband* or the word *father* either. To try. To heal the night or day. I'm busy selling fighters and bombers. The NASDAQ moves in my face. I'm wired to my greasy self-portrait. Every day in every way. America equals ghost. The wrong side of history. Flat matted yellow weeds. Who could believe "God chose me." Flat matted yellow weeds. God chose? You were dying that spring. Reading at some college I saw ROTC boys in fatigues. The talkiness of winter unwraps me now. In each room someone is fingering her or his soul. The talkiness of winter unwraps me now. The garden made unknowing by the snow. Erased by snow. Erased by snow. Two blocks from campus, a boy, maybe ten or eleven, yelled at a junior-high-school girl: "Ho-bag, incest baby, spread your legs." It's all naked out here. Nothing is here. It's all one big strip mall. We have a Ponderosa.

3

faith and rain
  brightness falls

  blank as glass
    brightness falls

Won't be the magic
lantern or dancer.
Won't be despite
the fullness of time,
the other three magic ones.
Won't be a year. Won't be a song.
Won't be a beginning.
Won't be forward.
Won't be on the way.
Won't be a dreary prison.
Won't be the month of May.
Won't be Mary. Won't be the sea road.
Won't be stronger.
Won't be younger.
Won't be pink. Won't be opening from under.

The word.
      The word of God.

The word of God
      in a plastic bag.

I couldn't hear.
      I couldn't hear

your voice.
      You are with me

and I shatter
      everyone who

hates you.
      Arrows on water;

you are with me—
      rain on snow—

and I shatter
      everyone who

hates you.
      faith and rain

brightness falls
      blank as glass

      brightness falls

SOUL-MAKING

as if that plain fact were enough and would last:
as if that plain fact were a fact not a sky:
as if a green sky were a fact not a face:
as if that plain face were a sky and enough:
as if that green sky were a face and would
speak:

When I close my eyes I see cracks in storm windows; there's a book on a bench near the flat small river, there's a cup of coffee on the bench. Let my soul be a sphere, let devotion move my soul. I think a sparrow might be a picture of death. I think I should make fun of myself. I think I can't hear you anymore. I think this is a bad day but you never say *the worst day.* I think I've fallen out of my chair. I think I was never fooling anyone—

A slow

embrace,
        mud-slick, salty—

thick ropes

of light,
        a painting forgetting

everything

but your mouth—

I can't turn off the engine. I just can't find the stamina to be a
squirrel anymore; I don't have the patience to mug myself in
Chagall after Chagall after Chagall; I don't have the helium to rise
and float above the town the way I used to; I don't have the broom
to sweep Orion into the water; I don't have the studio; I don't have
the world; I don't have the phone number; I don't have the book
of spells—

for I am

bodiless and bright:
my soul is like a green used car:

my soul is like a dancing bear,
an old drunk king, a patch of ice

CY TWOMBLY

You are getting it and you are getting it

here or there or somewhere you are seeming or you are seeming
  here or

there or somewhere this is the situation from which this derives
  find it here

and you are getting it and you are getting it here or there or
  somewhere

this is the generation or this is the transformation what if they
cannot find

here or there or sunset suggested projected provoked one-way
ticket the

sweetest songs in the words you have become them one-way
ticket or this

is the transformation is wonder

to be included and insulted cold gray sky on the first of
    December my soul

made a home in you for a while for long enough and it was all I
    could have

hoped for cold gray sky on the first of December you became a
    dry face

where I looked for and found dry compassion for a while for
    long enough

and it was all I could have hoped for to be included or insulted
    to live here

and not call it a waste land to live here to be included and
    insulted and not

to hear any misery in the sound of the wind

and not to hear any misery in the soul in the sky you

became a dirt face one must have a mind of winter and have
    been cold a long

time to be included and insulted cold gray sky I walked through
    snow to find

you I walked through sun to find you sunlight breaking glass
    bright trees

spinning in light I don't want to say good-bye to you I don't
    want to find your words I don't want to be dead I don't
    want to find your words torn up

inside my words I want to find thick ropes of light bright flat
    blue leaps

between elms

LITTLE LIGHTNING BOLT

Simon says, put your hands on your head.
Simon says, put your finger on your nose. Simon says, you haven't
done enough. Simon says, you don't care enough. Simon says,
compulsive old answers can't leave the world alone. Simon says,
you're going to die. Simon says, don't let yourself care. Simon says,
you can't stop caring. Simon says, man-tall but thin as a phone call,
compulsive old answers can't leave the world alone. Simon says, you
only have blood, marsh light, and sparrow. Simon says, put your
hands on your head—

THE HISTORY OF OUR DEATH

1

5/5/1944 LITZMANNSTADT-GHETTO

I have decided to write a diary, though it is a little too late. To reca-
pitulate past events is quite impossible, so I'll begin with the pres-
ent. This week I committed an act which best illustrates the degree
of "dehumanization" to which we have been reduced. I finished
my loaf of bread in three days, that is to say, on Sunday, so that I
had to wait till next Saturday for a new one. I was terribly hungry,
I had the prospect of living only on the workshop soups, which
consist of three little potato pieces and two dkg. of flour. Monday
morning I was lying quite dejectedly in my bed, and there was my
darling sister's half loaf of bread "present" with me. To cut a long
story short: I could not resist the temptation and ate it up totally.
After having done this—at present a terrible crime—I was over-
come by remorse of conscience and by a still greater care for what
my little one would eat the next five days. I felt like a miserable,
helpless criminal, but I was delivered from the situation by the
reception of a B-Allotment. I suffer, feigning that I don't know
where the bread has gone, and I have to tell people that it was
stolen by a supposed reckless and pitiless thief. And to keep up
appearances, I have to utter curses and condemnations of the
imaginary thief. "I would hang him with my own hands if I came
across him" and other angry phrases.

2

The top half

of a crab shell,
            thin as enamel

glaze, burnished
            ivory flecked

with purple,
            rough ovals,

half-ovals,
            hieroglyphs.

The shell,
            translucent,

has been cracked off
            at the bottom.

Green hair follicles
            are concentrated

around the holes
            where the face

once was.
            They made

us garbage—
  I was garbage—

they call me
  human garbage—

I *was* garbage
  so I still am—

—————————

Jew slave
  Jew slave

"Jew soup"
  Jew violence

dancing dancing
  hit them hit them

break them break them
  shrieking break them

the living know nothing
  I can't know

I read documents
  ("Jew slave"

"subhuman"
  "person without dignity")

in the winter light

3

Wavelets sound
　　like sheets

flapping.
　　A milk-thin clamshell

striped the brown of roots:
　　the rounded hinge inside

looks like a bone
　　inside a human ear

and the periwinkle
　　no bigger

than a hazelnut
　　in my palm

gives black, wet
　　invitations to the tongue.

Mussels, still closed,
　　alive, hold tight

to the oozy sand,
　　their green beards

trail beside them
　　in wetness, glinting.

The water now riled suede,
    a black cormorant flying.

I *was* garbage
    so I still am.

You loaned me
    your hair,

I lost it,
    he struck us down.

I burn for no
    reason, like

a lantern
    in daylight.

Orange light
    on the highway,

orange light
    on Rondo's Diner;

God breathing—
    in daughters and sons—

    God dancing—

I'LL FLY AWAY

                              he tried to give words away
he tried to pray—

obsessive compulsion is a disconnection between body
and mind, a situation of mutual distrust where all acts
are suspect and self-perception is unreliable—

                              one must have a mind of
summer, of water, of warm rain—his mind is winter,
copper, elegy, green silk, brown bread, dust—

obsessive compulsion is a disconnection between body
and mind, a situation of mutual distrust where all acts
are suspect and self-perception is unreliable—

                              one must have a mind of
distance, of marsh grass, of dead zones—his mind is
summer, wriggling, gulping, bouncing, form gulping
after formlessness: gray rain and buried worlds—

compulsive repetition usually implies a lack of
resolution between self and space

                              my friend is saying prayers
and saying prayers, there's nothing else—

PRAYER, BROKEN OFF

a stain of faded

storm light in my hand—

If I cried out,
Who among the angelic orders would
Slap my face, who would steal my
Lunch money, knock me
Down—sailboats moored
In harbor, trees on the long
Breakwater, orange shimmer
Of late July evening—I can't stop
Wanting the voice that will come—

2

Simon says, put your hands on your
head, Simon says, put your finger on your
nose, Simon says you haven't done enough,
Simon says you don't care enough, Simon
says, you can't stop caring—

Oh look at you—once again you're a
machine made of words, once again you're
a death, a failure, your responses always too
big and dirty
                          and you want them
to get bigger and dirtier—

3

to give
the storm a local
habitation and a name,
and small wind bring
down rain—echo and
window, self and all selves,
each day tears the air to
bits—and small wind bring
down rain—were you—did
that mirror, again, feed
you—when the moon rises,
black plums
taste like whiskey, pieces
of mirror

      sweep blue wind—

Two

FREE AGAIN

for Werner Sollors

FREE AGAIN

When I can't sleep I am full of red buds and torn curtains and shiny cars parked in a lot. My lower-middle-class manners tear through my upper-middle-class manners: I stared at braided colors in water while my peers figured out the art of the deal. I was (I wanted to be) a Midwestern boy with a disco in my eyes—Chicago Jew, greengolden suburb Jew, son of a Coney Island Jew. When I drank I got punched up by luminous waves of anger. I thought I had to choose between winning in New York and being a good person. I'm not a good person: a good person doesn't talk about himself—or so good people tell me. What is our country. Did it start as blank, as blank blank, as blank blank blank. I would love to fly to Vegas for the Punk Festival—we aren't the first culture to "monetize relationships"—force steel splintering, force breathing, moisture in the air: the city dissolves, one long story of corruption: USA means the outer miracle kills the inner miracle: history has to live with what was here: no images, no lightning, no letters of flame: leaves move, clouds move, money moves, night pushes through the money—

FREE AGAIN

                                    Toyota Camry, St. Mary's Laundry,
weeping beech, summer's end—

What was really going on—some creep couldn't hear my sense
of humor: now I'm wounded, I'm mouthwash, I'm cologne—

Outside the syllables, outside the grant proposal, I'm a
cracking song, a blighted meadow—

A city street, a baseball bat, a fashion spread, a vodka rocks—

FREE AGAIN

the elegies are taking off their clothes—

I can't make something out of nothing: Holiday Inn sign,
Independent Taxi—there are no symbols, no open roses hanging
down to the grass—shadow and wind, blue-gray car, bright red
car—there are no symbols, no spells—and water was my dirty name:
I'm just trying to make a night or a cathedral or a pine—why don't
people talk more about corporations and power—I'm just trying to
make midsummer night—she wants torn strips of city, she wants
wind and rain through torn strips of city—in the window a beadwork
Birth of Venus, beneath her a man sleeping in a doorway—voices
across the street: does that bar stay open—vcr sale $60—the
Dillinger 4, the Creeps, old Cocteau and Yeats in the window, a
picture of the green man—

FREE AGAIN

we need to know why voices fall apart—

we did so many things wrong—and all
our claims of innocence are false—and
sure we want to claim it—

we need to know which colors deer can
see—we need to know why voices fall
apart—a boy rode a swan, breathed a

peacock and a rat—

believe in the moon, believe
in Andy Warhol—

FREE AGAIN

You were born this year—maybe—I don't know your mother anymore, but I know who you are. Your life begins now. Will you look at your mother and say, "How could you be part of America—"

FREE AGAIN

We could just get lost in this hot day, in our wanting—we could just get lost—hot day, parking lot, dear friend on the phone but no one in the parking lot to make this day better—spotlight on Otis Redding, warm Wild Cherry Pepsi, sweet soul music, Archie Bell and the Drells—in the walk-in clinic on the Cartoon Network bear doctor examines elephant child—in the mall across the street from this mall, amazingly bad Kung Pao chicken—

Where am I equals who am I—does she like Southern Comfort through the snow—

FREE AGAIN
(IN PLACE OF A SELF)

"You've been disliked for three thousand years—do you ever look in the mirror"—stains on the wall, mattress on the floor, November night—nothing but the wild rain, orchard and branch, each kiss wanted raining—

God is spit on a windshield, ice on a sidewalk—"we have determined that you are different; we have decided that we will eat you—"

history (first draft): our cheap history keeps smiling—between the days somewhere—on the back of a receipt—

                              my handwriting, stories, Paul
                              Celan, phrases—

on the back of
        a receipt—
                somewhere

I made
        the words—angry
                enough—*pit*—

hot—pit—
        our
                cheap history
                keeps smiling—

                "you've been disliked
                for three thousand years:
                do you ever look in the mirror—"

FREE AGAIN

It could be gorgeous, it could be
loss, it could be broken, it could fold—

it could listen, it could stop, it
could answer, it could fail—

it could dangle, it could fall, it
could glisten, it could freeze—

the soul inventing the world—
the soul inventing the soul—

FREE AGAIN

Hi—

we're the middle class—venting:

collectors really began hounding us, but luckily our mom saw an
Oprah show about nonprofit debt management—what have you
seen—I can't answer—anything—these walls—holy garbage—
words and power and blinking lights—pieces of mirror sweep the
word: each step jiggles pink buildings—the Americans are here,
drunk on their own naughtiness—

> last night this wire
> trashcan made a torch—
> the Americans are
>   here, drunk on not
> having to
>   respond—

FREE AGAIN

                                    give the prince of business the
days of wine and roses—the smell of frost and coffee—don't be
absurd: you'll never meet princes of business—you don't know any
"upper-class" people—but you could just go to sleep, that would be
good—you could sleep here—you would be warm—

FREE AGAIN

He wants to apologize for the light
that's gone now, and the light that's coming next, and knowing it's
not news that no one in the story even *feels* innocent—he wants to
apologize for the cat on the restaurant patio, the half-naked friend
in bed with your dad, the night she slept with him wearing his
sweater, the snow falling outside the hot dog stand, the copy of
Baudelaire on the living room table—there are millions of suns
left—cat litter on wood steps, wood and tin mobile—stars fall down
the hall—

if anybody needs a branch in light,
if anybody needs the lake's glass skin—

FREE AGAIN

You never slept under a bridge—what blurs you—tell me common stories—there's a brownfield in Alma—petroleum processing—he says he'd rather work at 7-11 than live over there in Midland near all that stuff—you can smell it in the wind—

Letters shine outside "low-income housing"—there are arrows on the water—crab-apple-colored—thaw reaches up through mud,

                drenching wet opens stink,

            stains concrete moss-colored—

FREE AGAIN

The *Odyssey*, warehouses, snow,
power lines—dirt path, brown-green ice
between firs—

Choirs of repetition fired from graves—

"How do you know you're not
dead already"—

They thought they were freezing
so they set themselves on fire—tell me—
what did you witness—
What slipped through—

FREE AGAIN

We are ourselves because this is the world's first morning, and we are ourselves because it is not, and we are also not ourselves. I want you to stand there in your brightly frisky middle-class personalities and chant after me: "How about another tax cut, how about another tax cut—" "our wilderness" and liberty and justice for us: just equal the course of empire, the game of life—the self that wins and wins—American self, sleepy self—after night rain, sun pour through these chants—

America

named you, said you are "I": strip malls equal temples or clouds that drift to the words we can't speak—

singing hymns for no reason: and, and, and, and, and—I, I, I, I, I—

FREE AGAIN

what happened here—

      smell that stuff, moon near full, winter sun, yellow, winter
      trees, light on ice—Dow burns air—

      you say the sky, you think you mean the sky—

                    the sky betrays you when you say
the sky—

FREE AGAIN

        I remember that night, or
that night, or that afternoon; and all the while
tonight was ticking in the calendar. When we're
gone, our names will mean green body. When
we're gone, our names will mean green thought.
And we're afraid now, and thin snow is aiming
for the hole in each word. The promised
land—city of hope—MSNBC limo—you

        can sell your soul and
the nation profits—

FREE AGAIN

When no one else is watching—faith and night—when no one
else believes us—faith and night—

They are being washed in what they want—

In one hundred years we covered North America with concrete—

Beach houses, gray, tan, olive, in front of gold and orange
trees—before you sleep your lips will find unrest—

We are moving, swallowing pockets of garbage in our fat,
harvesting tumors—

Moon just before dawn—the road is gristle—pink kelp, yellow
reeds, green kelp—

Smokestacks the same gray as the low clouds—

FREE AGAIN

He visualized himself but he knew he was lying—he could
not make his life come true—his father hid pain in a pot
of gold, his mother hid pain in a hollow tree—he thought,
I'm just another St. Sebastian boy writhing—yum yum,
let's eat pain—Satan is the flip side of Jerry Falwell—
money shines body—glimpses of sex—the slightly drunk
wife in the kimono playacts for her lover—everything was
civilization—in the forest we can say anything that comes
to our minds and the words form shapes and flicker and
leap—choirs of repetition fired from graves—

FREE AGAIN

A dalmatian stands on a raised flower bed; green fell apart, green wanted to pray. And one night, one cold sky, one walking home, now one night in October, a million years too late, you glance at two kissing in front of the house, in the light in the driveway—they're spilling from houses and yards. A dirty wallet, a glass of wine, the dew on your gym shoes, a man drunk and a woman drunk, walking in the parking lot, coltish, then, just as fast, self-contained, inside, walking like sex in the parking lot. Who are your senses—who is your darkness—who is your wilderness—

FREE AGAIN

        Why don't people
tell the truth—you scare people—genocide and
how the rich got rich—even a bus shines
differently in the light, the glowing
splinters—why don't people talk more about
the government and power—how do I know
the rich can't sleep—promise me the rich can't
sleep—

FREE AGAIN

        Stillness in red, stillness in green—I
have no words, light hangs like rope—

        We breathe our eyes, promise the
wind, boxes of shit, pieces of glass—

        Color the wind, we breathe our yes,
open the doors, one vote one corpse—

        One seed of light—

FREE AGAIN

The I feels grateful for its bagel, grateful for its espresso—
now try it this way: the I lives in an empire—community
of headlines, community of video loops—all its friends
feel terrible— "guilt is the new terrorism—"

       the Dostoevsky Network: all writhing,
       all the time—

FREE AGAIN

*in the sweet exhale of July where dead
zones pock the mind just west of the end of the world where the
local lost boy nailed dogs to the walls of his shack where the
headless ghost dogs run through the waste where brownfields
and toxic emissions give extra laughter its oily shine black
water moving between pines the foundation of a house*

FREE AGAIN

                    boats in the harbor, fog burning
off Mt. Tam—what—*exactly*—did I promise you—

                    money has won everywhere,
money has won—says some bigshot—

                    I don't—I don't want to admit it—
look into the face—ownership is twice as smug here—

                    past Sausalito, past light in fir trees, past gold hills
slipping down—the water and the fog and the
barges, the Golden Gate,

                    a city, a game, a pyramid
scheme—stop, pay toll—gift center—

                    to prevent theft, lock doors—

FREE AGAIN

like anyone else, we had our shattered selves—like anyone else—
we owe ourselves and all we are to death—

       a light bulb fails, and each town fills
and empties, empties and fills—

       this town could be Eden, for us—the freedom of
each one—this is God risen—I was a rock star, a shaman, a
buffoon, a hero—

       each of these experiences was very
good for me—

       I have an indomitable will to win—like true love, I
conquer all—like death and mirrors, I am certain—

       it's all within my reach—

FREE AGAIN

        In the fall of a sparrow—late light—for you—
the readiness is all—

I have a gun in my head—it costs one thin dime—matter is water
(I noticed)—when the child is trying to speak, trying to tell about
the house—the house, the woman, the rivulet in the forest—there
is no nature—they were in a cab in the forest—they were in a bar
in the forest—how do you become a flat lake—the lake could not
answer—I am a lake and sometimes I can dip my hand in—the
child listens to the crows dying in the street—blue night—he was
too young to say blue night is so tired—we drove through the
layers of color, the textures—I want two blue sleeping pills—

        I can remember my secret book—
I was a ghost, you were the only one

        who could hear me—

NOTES

"'Broken World' (For James Assatly)":

When I met James Assatly in 1991, he was completing his novel *Hejira*. By the spring of 1992, when he graduated from Brown with his MFA, James had grown increasingly ill and was living at home with his parents. In 1993 he died in Boston of an AIDS-related illness. In an interview, Edmund White, with whom James worked closely at Brown, called *Hejira* a "remarkable novel . . . As long as *we* live," White said, "*we'll* remember that book." I wrote this poem to honor James and his book, and to mourn all the words and worlds that were lost when we lost him. He was one of the smartest, toughest, most gifted people I knew then or have known since. He died on the morning of his thirty-first birthday—March 25, 1993. His novel remains unpublished.

"The History of Our Death":

I quote from *"Les Vrais Riches"—Notizen am Rand: Ein Tagebuch aus dem Ghetto Lódź (Mai bis August 1944)*, eds. Hanno Loewy and Andrzej Bodek (Leipzig: Reclam Verlag, 1997).

"I'll Fly Away":

I quote from Celeste Olalquiaga's *Megalopolis: Contemporary Cultural Sensibilities* (University of Minnesota Press, 1992).

"Prayer, Broken Off":

The phrase "small wind bring down rain" comes from a poem by Suzanne Keen; Keen's source is "Western Wind."

COLOPHON

Broken World was designed at Coffee House Press,
in the historic warehouse district of downtown Minneapolis.
Fonts include Minion and Antique Olive.

FUNDER ACKNOWLEDGMENT

Coffee House Press is an independent nonprofit literary publisher. Our books are made possible through the generous support of grants and gifts from many foundations, corporate giving programs, individuals, and through state and federal support. This book has received special project support from the National Endowment for the Arts, a federal agency. Coffee House Press receives general operating support from the Minnesota State Arts Board, through an appropriation by the Minnesota State Legislature and from the National Endowment for the Arts, and major general operating support from the McKnight Foundation, and from the Target Foundation. Coffee House also receives support from: an anonymous donor; the Elmer and Eleanor Andersen Foundation; the Buuck Family Foundation; the Patrick and Aimee Butler Family Foundation; Gary Fink; Stephen and Isabel Keating; the Lenfesty Family Foundation; Ethan James Litman; Rebecca Rand; the law firm of Schwegman, Lundberg, Woessner & Kluth, P.A.; the James R. Thorpe Foundation; the Archie D. and Bertha H. Walker Foundation; Thompson West; the Woessner Freeman Family Foundation; Wood-Rill Foundation; and many other generous individual donors.

This activity is made possible in part by a grant from the Minnesota State Arts Board, through an appropriation by the Minnesota State Legislature and a grant from the National Endowment for the Arts.

MINNESOTA
STATE ARTS BOARD

NATIONAL
ENDOWMENT
FOR THE ARTS

To you and our many readers across the country,
we send our thanks for your continuing support.

Good books are brewing at coffeehousepress.org

JOSEPH LEASE is the author of two critically acclaimed collections of poetry: *Human Rights* and *The Room*. His poems have also been featured on NPR and published in *The AGNI 30th Anniversary Poetry Anthology, VQR, Bay Poetics, Paris Review,* and elsewhere. The title poem from this collection, "'Broken World' (For James Assatly)," appeared in *The Best American Poetry,* edited by Robert Creeley and David Lehman. Thomas Fink's book *A Different Sense of Power: Problems of Community in Late-Twentieth-Century U.S. Poetry* includes extensive critical analysis of Lease's poetry.

Originally from Chicago, Lease lives in Oakland, California and chairs the MFA Program in Writing at California College of the Arts in San Francisco.